RENDEZVOUS

A 21-Day Encounter with the King

JOAN HOOD

Copyright

Rendezvous

By Joan Hood

Editing by Jim Bryson (JamesLBryson@Gmail.com)

Contents

INTRODUCTION

Hello Friends! Welcome to my world!

The following pages are purely a result of my RENDEZVOUS with God. I learned a lifestyle of encounters with God at a young age. Through many life events and circumstances, including the "unwanted" ones, God was faithful to speak, lead and guide me, even when I was unaware.

For years, I kept all these "citas" (Spanish for "appointments" or "dates") with God to myself. They were, and still are, very private and intimate interactions with God. Here lately, the Lord has been speaking to me about sharing them with those who would welcome raw, matter-of-fact encounters with Him.

My prayer is that you will glean from these precious encounters with God. And when you finish the last page, you find yourself more in love with Jesus, singing Him praises even at the oddest times, purposely living only for Him and doing His Kingdom assignment over your life.

I included some notes and guidelines on the 21-Day Daniel Fast, as most of these encounters are a direct outcome during a fast. May your fasting be defining!

Carpe Diem – Seize the Day! The days God ordained for you. Stop. Look. Listen. Slow down or speed it up. How ever the Lord is leading you. Just so you're doing precisely what He has called you to do. And all, as a result of your rendezvous with the King!

Siempre y para siempre!

(Always & Forever)

To The King!

Joan

DAY 1

You are my hiding place;
You keep me from trouble;
You surround me with
Songs of deliverance. *Selah*

Psalm 32:7

Stop striving and know that I am God;
I will be exalted among the nations
I will be exalted on the earth.

Psalm 46:10

MY HIDING PLACE

Hide and Seek was one popular game that a once a little girl like me used to play with my siblings and friends growing up. Not being found was my high, and I always had a knack for finding obscure places to hide. Finding and outing me was like hitting a Jackpot in the lottery. It suddenly became everyone's pursuit to see me first; then, everybody wanted to do something different afterward.

Finding my hiding spot in God took me a while in my faith walk. Or I should say, my hiding place *is* God. I thought a place of security is where you arrive at a certain height or accomplishments earning a degree, a big house, nice cars, money in the bank, a good family, social status, etc. But even in all of that, life wasn't absent of troubles and a number of life-altering situations I had to overcome.

I realized that my place of safety is God—His presence. The calm that He provides and the sanity He gives in times of emotional and psychological warfare are unmatched. I don't have to drive to a church building or call the prayer line (although there is nothing wrong with calling for prayer). Right where I am, I pause and sit quietly in Him. Everything else fades away. Then, I catch myself humming away a song that He gives me in my moment of silence.

Sometimes, that's all it takes. Be quiet. Silence the many voices that are nagging in your ears or mind. Allow His peace to come. He'll speak to you and help you navigate through your circumstances—no big hoopla. Just go to Him and hide in Him when life's troubles want to find you out.

When the load gets heavy, and you feel like running to hide, know that God's presence is the best and safest place to hide!

Let's Pray

Father, thank you for letting me hide in You. When my goings get tough and I find myself ready to give up, I pray You hold me close and remind me that I can run to You and find my refuge in You. May this be my resolve and ever be my anchor—You are my hiding place, and I am safe in You! Thank you, Father.

Our Decree

I decree that my awareness of the presence of God is ever-increasing in my life, and that running to Him remains my only option and nothing else.

I decree every counterfeit affection is uprooted and forever dismissed in my life. This I decree in Yeshua's name. Amen.

DAY 2

I will instruct you and teach you
In the way which you should go;
I will advise you with My eye upon you.

Psalm 32:8

Make sure that your character is free from the love of money, being content with what you have; for He Himself has said, "I will never desert you, nor will I ever abandon you,"

Hebrews 13:5

Also see Psalm 121

EYES THAT SEE ME THROUGH

I never looked into the story behind the song "Somebody's Watching Me." I'm not sure if I want to. Listening to the song (not on purpose) gives me the weebie-jeebies. It's freaky.

With God, however, I take comfort in knowing that He is watching me constantly. He watches my goings and my comings. As long as I remain conscious of His presence, I can feel His eyes watching me, especially in my travels overseas. There's nothing like knowing Father is watching me! His eyes are my constant companion.

He does more than watch; He counsels with His eyes. What does that even mean? The word *counsel* in Hebrew is *yaats* and it means "advise (verb), conspire, planned, purposed." This word has many other meanings but is similar and interconnected. But notice how these words are action words and are intentional.

This reminds me of Psalm 121:5 &10. God is relentless in watching over His children. He makes sure we stay the course.

This reminds me of Micah's football games when he was younger. Greg would be on the sidelines, running at Micah's speed and cheering him on to ensure he got to the other end or accomplished what he needed to do for that particular play.

We have such a bad habit of being unaware of God's presence—the Immanuel, the God who is ever present, the One who promises never to leave us nor forsake us (ref. Hebrews 13:5). We need to kick this bad habit quickly and realize that God keeps watch over us all the time. Not with stationary eyes, but with eyes that make sure we make it through!

I pray this becomes your song as well:

> Let us become more aware of Your presence.
> Let us experience the glory of Your goodness.

(Song: *Holy Spirit, You Are Welcome Here*)

Let's Pray

Father, I pray that Your loving eyes see me through my internal struggles. Not just to overcome momentarily but to learn to be aware that Your eyes are on me constantly.

Thank you, that I can rest assured that Your powerful love is committed to bringing me into wholeness.

Thank you for Your faithfulness, even when I am unaware. Teach me and show me Your ways.

I pray this in Jesus' name. Amen.

Our Decree

I decree God's faithfulness is seen around the globe in greater measure through me.

I declare my eyes are enlightened to the truth that God's eyes have remained on us since the beginning of time.

This I decree in Yeshua's name. Amen.

DAY 3

The sorrows of the wicked are many,
But the one who trusts in the Lord,
Goodness will surround him.

Psalm 32:10

Trust in the Lord with all your heart
And do not lean on your own understanding.
In all your ways acknowledge Him,
And He will make your paths straight.

Proverbs 3:5-6

TRUST IN THE LORD WITH ALL YOUR HEART

If you know anything about me, that song *Trust In The Lord With All Your Heart* that Don Moen made popular in the early 90s should already be ringing in your ears. That song has been my constant companion, especially in my travels. Back when I started traveling at age 17, due to the unknown variables of travel at a very young age, I would make an intentional effort to remind myself that I could trust the Lord AT ALL TIMES, regardless of where I was or what I was facing.

I was deployed as a missionary to Tarlac—a province in the Northern part of the Philippines, with another young lady from our church. I was mentally scared because I was unfamiliar with the place (Google was not a thing back in the late 80s); plus, I didn't speak their dialect.

The over two months of trodding unfamiliar places for the sake of the Gospel was, needless to say, the most unnerving experience in my younger life. Consequently, it turned out to be the beginning of a lifestyle of rendezvous with God. From *Through it All*:

> I've learned to trust in Jesus
> I've learned to trust in God

Those precious two months shaped my heart and mind to wholly lean on the Lord in times of uncertainty. Mind you, back then, there were no cell phones or social media to keep my family abreast of how I was. I praise God even more for my parents' faith in God and trust in me.

I came home speaking (and, you guessed it, singing) in Ilocano—that region's dialect and my Dad's! Growing up, I dreaded going to my Dad's relatives' place because I didn't speak the dialect. It felt good to make my Daddy proud coming home from a Mission trip!

Obeying and trusting God have perks! It's always a win-win with God!

Let's Pray

Father, I thank You for You are trustworthy.

Thank You for the many times You have kept me in close proximity to You, even at a young age.

Thank you for allowing me to experience You and for helping me learn from unnecessary things or mistakes I've made.

Thank you for being lavish in Your love and Your grace.

Thank you for the confidence You put inside me when things are uncertain. May I never lose my wonder.

This I pray in Jesus' name. Amen.

Our Decree

I decree that God's unmatched faithfulness reverberates around the globe.

I decree the dismantling of every doubt and every fear over God's ability to perform in times of uncertainty.

I decree hope is arising and faith increasing in the one, true God, Yeshua Hamashiach!

This I decree in His name, Amen.

DAY 4

The steps of a man are established by the Lord,
And He delights in his way.
When he falls, he will not be hurled down,
Because the Lord is the One who holds his hand.
I have been young and now I am old,
Yet I have not seen the righteous forsaken
Or his descendants begging for bread.
All day long he is gracious and lends,
And his descendants are a blessing.

Psalm 37:23-26

The sorrows of the wicked are many,
But the one who trusts in the Lord
Goodness will surround him.

Psalm 32:10

HE HOLDS MY HAND

We could say much about "holding hands" and what it means to an individual or a culture. Or even what a hand represents.

Being held is a powerful thing. As a child growing up, it meant love, acceptance and security to me. I remember faking a fall from my bed at around 4 years old. I may have had a bad dream that I just felt like being held by my Dad. My culture is not touchy-touchy. We were not even verbal with our affections. I never heard "I love you" growing up. So, for me to fake a fall so my Dad would hold me says a lot. I remember what it felt like. How comforting and secure I felt when he held me and hushed me from crying.

That feeling of security carried over when I got married. I married one of the most loving individuals I've ever known. Greg is not shy about Personal Displays of Affection (PDAs), especially when hugging and holding my hands. It is one of the dearest things I miss when I'm traveling without him.

Imagine God holding you! Being held by the One who is steady and steadfast. One whom we can rely on at ALL times! One who supports and sustains us at whatever time. *Samak* is the Greek for "hold;" it also means "to uphold, support, and rest." What a God! No wonder David stayed pretty confident and didn't shy about resting on Him when facing terrifying battles, even fighting himself as his enemy!

Find confidence in knowing that God holds you at whatever time! Allow Him to display His love toward you by welcoming His hand v.25 displays David's confidence in that knowing God is faithful. Don't make that a cliché; make it a reality.

I could hear the song *Confidence* sung by Chris Tomlin. I particularly love the part that says,

> I will rest in Your promises
> My confidence is Your faithfulness

May you rest in His loving arms that hold you even when you're unaware.

Let's Pray

Father, teach me to lean on You continually, at all times, even at reasonable times. Teach me to be thankful and to always look towards knowing You more and more.

This I pray in Jesus' name. Amen.

Our Decree

I decree that confidence in God becomes a reality for every person on this planet!

This I decree in Yeshua's name. Amen.

DAY 5

Make me know Your ways, Lord;
Teach me Your paths.

Psalm 25:4

Teach me Your way, Lord;
I will walk in Your truth;
Unite my heart to fear Your name.

Psalm 86:11

The plans of the heart belong to a person,
But the answer of the tongue is from the Lord.

Proverbs 16:1

Also see Proverbs 16:1-9

NOW WHAT?

Have you ever been in a place of "I got it all together,"
and suddenly, all your plans started to not make sense?
You spent all this time planning and putting things in

23

place, only to realize the square peg does not fit in the round hole.

Shaking off what has been and what we reckoned to be what should be, is like pulling teeth with no anesthesia. I know that it is painful to even think about, but the Church was, and still is (to a significant degree), in that state when God began to confront the spirit of religion. "Hard to break a habit," we resign to say sometimes as an excuse. But like Pop (my father-in-law) used to say, "Get 'er done!"

I could hear Solomon screaming, "God gives the final answer." It would save us years of our lives and money if we heed to v.1 of Proverbs 16. We can make plans however we want to. We can make it all savvy. We can even spend all our money in the bank if we want to. But unless it is in accordance with God's purpose in your life, we will find ourselves spinning our wheels but going nowhere.

Going around the mountain—same mountain, mind you—is no fun! How do we get 'er done?

Drop everything that's insanely producing the same result, and allow Holy Spirit to redirect you! It is humbling, but it will be the ONLY way to save you from missing your mark. I would rather push the restart button than act like I got it all together, only to find out I was nowhere near what God wanted me to do in my life.

I love to sing "Teach Me Your Ways," but it is the scariest feeling when I know I may have to begin again. But then again, with God, it is always a win-win! So, I choose to yield.

Let's Pray

Father, teach me to learn Your ways and be obedient. Forgive my stubbornness, and grace me to shift, change, adjust…how ever You see fit. I know that's scary even to say, but I'd rather be scared of changing than not progressing at all!

Open my understanding to grasp Your ways and teach me to lean on Your truth that makes me free.

This I pray in Yeshua's name. Amen.

Our Decree

I decree that the truth of God's word sets people free from the bondage of religion and human traditions.

This I decree in Yeshua's name. Amen.

DAY 6

Peace I leave you, My peace I give you; not as the world gives, do I give to you. Do not let your hearts be troubled, nor fearful.

John 14:27

Faithful is He who calls you, and He also will do it.

1 Thessalonians 5:24

Also see Mathew 14:22-33

EYES ON ME

Sometimes, God gives me a little tap on my shoulder and says, "Eyes on Me." It's so easy to get caught up in busyness—the many distractions (sometimes good ones, nevertheless, distractions) that sometimes keep us off kilter.

Sometimes, it's not sin that keeps us "away" from God but the shift in our focus. I sometimes dabble with cameras and almost always adjust the lenses to get the desired result. More often than not, because I can't stay still, I mess up the focus, which results in blurry images.

Sometimes, keeping it simple to keep the main thing the *main* thing is what it all takes to keep your momentum going. Sometimes, in victory, confetti is not necessary.

Peter was doing well and experienced the supernatural of walking on water. He did more than the others. Peter was the courageous one. But as soon as he took his eyes off Jesus, he started sinking. Fear began to envelop him. Jesus had to come to his rescue.

Sometimes, you feel surrounded and overwhelmed with the tasks (they can be good ones), or you feel like you are drowning in too much care in the world: bills to pay, sickness, unfavorable circumstances within your family relationships. Whatever that may be. Remember to keep your eyes on Him. Sometimes, that's all it takes—your eyes on Him—the One who called you and the One who is capable of calming the waves or the storms in your life.

Turn your eyes upon Jesus
Look full in His wonderful face
And the things of earth will grow strangely dim

In the light of His glory and grace.

Hey, eyes on Him!

Let's Pray

Father, help me be single-hearted towards You; that my sole propensity is to trust You when I get overwhelmed. May Holy Spirit remind me of Your careful hands tapping me on my shoulder when I veer off the path You designed for me.

Give me the strength, Lord Jesus, to push me to the finish line and to never give up.

May I never lose the wonder of Your grace.

This I pray in Yeshua's name. Amen.

Our Decree

I decree the mercy of God prevails over every difficult thing the earth is experiencing today.

This I decree in Yeshua's name. Amen.

DAY 7

As for God, His way is blameless;
The word of the Lord is refined;
He is a shield to all who take refuge in Him.

Psalm 18:30

From the sons of Issachar, men who understood
the times, with knowledge of what Israel should
do, their chiefs were two hundred; and all their
kinsmen were at their command.

1 Chronicles 12:32

Also see 1 Samuel 3:1-11

RECONOCER (RECOGNIZE)

I was recently in Costa Rica to teach at our Kingdom
University campus in San Rafael de Heredia. As an
agreement with our host church, whoever comes to
teach would stay over to preach or minister on that
Sunday. A few minutes before I went up, I heard the

word *reconocer*. I had no earthly idea what it meant. I leaned over to my interpreter, who gently told me it meant "recognize." Well, this is one of those moments where God interrupted my flow, if you know what I mean. (We preachers run into this trouble a lot. LOL!)

Well, there are two things I learned about divine interruptions like this.

One: immediately yield to the prompting of Holy Spirit, or you could quickly make a fool of yourself.

Two: make the necessary adjustments and trust God to help you deliver this new revelation because, trust me, He knows best!

God had to call Samuel four times before recognizing it was God calling him and not Eli. Of course, Eli had to help him recognize God's voice. Nevertheless, God was speaking, and Samuel needed to hear Him.

We often fumble in life because we do not recognize God's careful instructions. We usually go about our program and our desired plans and ideas, our customary daily routine, and fail to acknowledge God's gentle whispers. More often than not, all we care about is "my way or the highway." Perhaps we end our day singing Frank Sinatra's *My Way*, blasting it with "I Did It My Way!"

Being stubborn can be a good asset if used in a good way. That was almost the nickname my mother gave me growing up. I praise God we can be pliable in His careful hands. He speaks, we listen!

Let's Pray

Father, I ask for Your grace to keep me pliable and teachable. Forgive my stubbornness!

May my ears be attentive to Your voice and my heart be ready to obey.

This I pray in Yeshua's name. Amen.

Our Decree

I decree that we cease striving and quickly recognize that God constantly speaks to help us navigate this life according to His design.

This I decree in Yeshua's name. Amen.

DAY 8

The fig tree has ripened its fruit,
And the vines in blossom have
Given forth their fragrance.
Arise, my darling, my beautiful one,
And come along!

Song of Solomon 2:13-14

After these things I looked, and behold, a door standing open in heaven, and the first voice which I had heard, like the sound of a trumpet speaking with me, said, "Come up here, and I will show you what must take place after these things."

Revelation 4:1

DANCE WITH ME

I was invited to an early morning prayer gathering in town, which women mostly attended. There was an immediate legislative argument inside of me because if you know anything about me, it has to take an act of Congress for me to attend these kinds of meetings. I didn't mind the "7:30 am early part." It was the "women" part that called a special session in my brain. My heart and my brain were in immediate conflict.

But it was one of those moments where I knew in my knower I had to go. Of course, I'm new in town, and I didn't know anybody from Adam except for the one who invited me and maybe a couple of others. The venue was magnificent—a massive house they turned into a gathering place.

As soon as I walked in, I could not deny the sweet presence of God in the room. The keyboard player freely played some familiar songs—no voice, just the keys. I grabbed a chair by a massive column, closed my eyes, and minded my business.

I hummed the song that was playing:

> Won't You Dance with me,
> O Lover of my soul
> To the song of all songs?
> Romance me,
> O Lover of my soul
> To the song of all songs.
> *Dance with Me* by Jesus Culture

I was caught up at a moment in time when I felt I was in another dimension—a heavenly realm. It was an unexplainable space in time, yet it felt so tangible. I didn't know how long I was there when a lady who recognized me elbowed me.

I was slightly annoyed because I didn't want to leave that realm, that moment, that experience. I may have even given her a fake smile to tell you the truth. But the Lord quickly whispered, "You (can) live in both realms."

Those were the most powerful words I had heard in a long time! Now I know why I came! That day is forever etched in the core of my being. That began a pursuit to dance with God—to rendezvous with Him—every chance I get.

"Present yourself," "show up," or "to get yourself to a (place)" are a few literal meanings of the French word *rendezvous*. I chuckled because I realized there was no date or appointment unless I showed up. I discovered the Lord is just waiting for us to meet Him so He can share His heart, desires, and plans with us. This is a secret He wants us to discover. A date with Him; a place where we find our surety.

Don't stand Him up!

Let's Pray

Father, I thank You for making it possible for us to see You manifest in the seen realm.

Thank you for not being bound by time and space.

Thank you for being willing to rendezvous with us forever.

May I continue to love to dance with You.

This I pray in Yeshua's name. Amen.

Our Decree

I decree that the Ekklesia is constant in her pursuit to rendezvous with the King!

I decree the rhythm of God's heart is manifested in the earth and the lives of His people.

This I decree in Yeshua's name. Amen.

DAY 9

Read these: Psalms 16, 23, 63

I CAN'T LIVE (IF LIVING IS WITHOUT YOU)

I left that morning prayer gathering so pumped and ready to conquer the world! I felt like I had stepped on a landmine, and I didn't mind it blowing me to pieces. I found joy. I found peace. I found a new meaning for existence. This Kingdom living is fun!

While driving to another meeting, I caught myself singing at the top of my lungs. I was getting with it since I was the only one in the car. I cried; I worshiped; I prayed and made decrees. Honestly, I don't know how I managed to keep my eyes on the road! That was one of those memorable times in the Lord.

Sitting at a red light, singing so loud, I realized I was jigging with Mariah Carey's *Without You*. ("I Can't Live, If Living is Without You.") I was boohooing like nobody's business! I was singing to God, telling Him how much I loved Him and that He was the reason for my living.

Then suddenly, I snapped out of that moment and realized: *Oh no! I am singing a secular song to God!*

See how quickly that religious spirit ruins moments like that? I did apologize if I was singing an inappropriate song, but the Lod assured me that He loved my singing, that the world brought perversion to music, and that it was time to redeem it. Boom! What a God!

Again, it's a win-win with God! I love it when we can simply be in God. No act. Just be.

Sing to Him a love song. He'll love it!

Let's Pray

Father, thank You for the simplicity of the joy You bring.

Thank you for loving us and allowing us to enjoy the uniqueness of how You created us.

Thank You for allowing me to sing back to You because I know You sing to me all the time.

May my song always be "I can't live without You."

This I pray in Yeshua's name. Amen.

Our Decree

I decree joy returning as we learn to dance with the joy-giver!

This I decree in Yeshua's name. Amen.

DAY 10

Mary said, "Behold, the Lord's bond-servant; may it be done to me according to your word." And the angel departed from her.

Luke 1:38

The steps of a man are established by the Lord, And He delights in his way.

Psalm 37:23

Also see Psalm 37

AVEC AISLES

The way God deals with me sometimes is that He would randomly speak some funny words or phrases just out of the blue.

I was emptying my dishwasher while thinking and praying for my upcoming Costa Rica trip when I heard Him say, "Avec aisles."

43

Of course, I have no clue what it meant, much less know how to pronounce it. So, I kept it on the back burner, thinking it might be for the France trip, not the Costa Rica trip.

During the previous months, I had a conversation with one of our Pastors in Costa Rica, and they mentioned a poor fishing village called Costa de Pajaros. I had developed a desire and a burden to reach out to this community with an outreach, initially thinking about doing a medical mission concurrent with a kids' camp.

I carried that burden in my heart for several months to allow God to drop clear directives on how to put the vision into action. A few months later, I was slated to teach at Kingdom University – Costa Rica, and I made it a point to scout the place for the planned outreach.

Standing in the middle of the field on the prospective venue of the outreach, we prayed and sought the Lord and made decrees. While praying, I heard it again, loud and clear: "Avec aisles."

With curiosity piqued, I asked the locals what *pajaros* meant. Happily, they retorted, "With wings!"

I quickly Googled "Avec Aisles" in French. Nobody can make this stuff up. It means "with wings!" After picking up my jaw from the floor, I knew God was undoubtedly giving me a thumbs up on a planned outreach. And yes, you guessed it—we are doing it, and it's just a matter of when.

It may seem obscure to us when God randomly speaks. It may be because we cannot place it or connect it to something we already know or are familiar with. But it will help tremendously if we just let it simmer and allow God to break it down for us. God does nothing without a reason or a purpose. When He speaks, we need to listen. It may not make sense then, but guaranteed, He will make sense of it when the time is ripe.

When He speaks to you, pay attention!

Let's Pray

Father, teach us to pay attention to Your voice. May we always be conscious of Your voice because You speak all the time. I pray to remain thankful for the many times You have affirmed and confirmed what You have put in my heart to do.

Thank You for not running out of ideas and ways to let us know You are near. I love You, Father.

This I pray in Yeshua's name. Amen.

Our Decree

I decree that our ears are attentive to the voice of God so that we will accomplish what He has already declared over us and all He has called us to do.

This I decree in Yeshua's name. Amen.

DAY 11

You will know the truth, and the truth will set you free.

John 8:32

It was for freedom that Christ set us free; therefore keep standing firm and do not be subject again to a yoke of slavery.

Galatians 5:1

For the kingdom of God is not eating and drinking, but righteousness and peace and joy in the Holy Spirit.

Romans 14:17

Also see Luke 22:29-32

KINGDOM IS TRUTH; RELIGION IS LIE

Over the past 15 I years, I have become disgusted with religion. I feel I have been duped into believing a lie about Christianity or this thing called the Church. We have relegated the King and His domain into this religious mumbo-jumbo we call Christianity. We have become too lazy to study the Word of God ourselves and too passive to confront the lies.

Religion (traditions of man) water down the Word of God and renders it with no effect (Mark 7:13). Religion sucks! Stay away from it! You should consider enrolling at Kingdom University.

For more info, email Office@kingdomu.org

The below narrative has reinforced my pursuit to rediscover the Kingdom of God. (I don't know who wrote it or even remember where I found it. Whoever you are, thank you for saying it, and sorry, I didn't know where to ask permission to use it).

Truth and Lie

The Lie said to the Truth, "Let's take a bath together; the well water is very nice."

The Truth was suspicious, tested the water and found it really nice. So, they got naked and bathed.

Suddenly, the Lie leaped out of the water and fled wearing the clothes of the Truth. The Truth, furious, climbed out of the well to get her clothes back.

But the World, upon seeing the naked Truth, looked away with anger and contempt. Poor Truth returned to the well to hide her shame and disappeared forever.

Since then, the Lie runs around the world dressed as the Truth, and society is happy because the world has no desire to know the naked Truth.

Let's Pray

Father, I pray for the truth of Your word to illuminate this darkened world.

I pray that You open our eyes to see the truth and for freedom to ring in the hearts and minds of the people.

I pray for increased discernment for the truth to strip naked the lies propagating in this world.

I declare freedom over every encumbering lie and bondage that has engulfed humanity for generations.

I declare metanoia (repentance) to manifest over the minds and hearts of Your people, the Church.

This I pray in Yeshua's name. Amen.

Our Decree

I decree that Light dispels darkness! I decree the father of Lies is forever bound in Heaven and Earth. I decree freedom ringing in the hearts and minds of God's people.

This I decree in Yeshua's name. Amen.

Day 12

If you will listen carefully to the voice of the Lord your God, and do what is right in His sight, and listen to His commandments, and keep all His statutes, I will put none of the diseases on you which I have put on the Egyptians; for I, the Lord, am your healer.

Exodus 15:26

But He was pierced for our offenses,
He was crushed for our wrongdoings;
The punishment for our well-being
Was laid upon Him,
And by His wounds we are healed.

Isaiah 53:5

And while being abusively insulted, He did not insult in return; while suffering, He did not threaten, but kept entrusting Himself to Him who judges righteously; and He Himself brought our sins in His body up on the cross, so that we might die to sin and live for righteousness; by His wounds you were healed.

1 Peter 2:23-24

ALL MEANS ALL

One day, I was praying for a dear friend who was battling cancer. He didn't get a good doctor's report, but it didn't faze him. It drove him to fight against the doctors' negative yet possibly factual reports and instead believed what God had written in His word concerning healing. That "fight" in him ignited a healing movement across the nations and around the world.

While praying, I heard Holy Spirit say, "I am the same God you believe for your salvation, that made provisions for your healing." I had a short "aha" moment there and conversed with myself: "If I can believe God to save my soul, why can't I believe Him for healing or any other thing I need?"

In the early part of last year, while emptying my dishwasher (my best place to hear God!), I heard the Lord say audibly: "I will heal your knees."

I was stunned for a second because it was clearly a voice I heard, and I didn't have issues with my knees.

A few months later, I was in Kenya and during the early part of the trip, I twisted my knee and tore my ACL. I experienced the most excruciating pain I've ever felt in my life. I have a very high pain tolerance, but this one got me. At night, while everyone else was sleeping, I was drowning in tears because of pain.

I was in the interior of Africa, so there was nothing there and nowhere to go to find relief. I brought some over-the-counter pain relievers, but they didn't work. I prayed, we prayed, and we went on with our mission. During the nights, pain would visit me and disrupt my rest.

But while the enemy thought he got me, I remembered what God had spoken to me audibly the previous months. I contended for that Word and chose to believe God.

I was still limping after a few days, even after we got home. It wasn't "normal" for a couple of months. Even some of my physical activities were impaired, but I kept contending.

A few weeks later, on another trip, I realized I wasn't limping. I wasn't hurting. My mobility was exceptional, even to this day! God healed me!

The same God who saves is the same God who heals, delivers, and provides for everything we need! He is our ALL in ALL, the great I AM! (ref. Isaiah 48:12; Exodus 3:14.)

All means All, y'all!

Let's Pray

Father, please remind me that You are an excellent God, and there is no shadow of turning with You!

You are constant and rich in mercy and love.

You encompass all knowledge and all authority known to man. Yet You are more than what we could ask or imagine.

You are our Father;

You are our source of everything.

May I never lose that wonder!

This I pray in Yeshua's name. Amen.

Our Decree

I decree that every known power and authority is unmatched against the power and authority of the true God Yeshua Hamashiach. There is only one God, and He owns everything!

This I decree in Yeshua's name. Amen.

DAY 13

From the sons of Issachar, men who understood the times, with knowledge of what Israel should do, their chiefs *were* two hundred; and all their kinsmen were at their command.

1 Chronicles 12:32

Behold, the former things have come to pass,
Now I declare new things;
Before they sprout, I proclaim them to you.

Isaiah 42:9

Behold, I am going to do something new,
Now it will spring up;
Will you not be aware of it?
I will even make a roadway in the wilderness,
Rivers in the desert.

Isaiah 43:19

WATCH FOR LANDMINES

My father trained me to watch beyond what physical eyes could see. I remember that growing up, he seemed to know some things that never crossed people's minds. He seemed to know what I had been up to while he was at work!

My curiosity was always piqued, and I developed a very inquisitive mind. (I was relieved to realize I wasn't the only one. David was too! He inquired of the Lord a lot! (ref. Psalm 34:4-8; 2 Samuel 21:1; Psalm 27:4-6).

And so, I've learned to watch to understand people's behavior. What's the method behind the madness? One day, one of my team members mentioned a timeline in her life and how she foresees the coming months to unfold for her. She said she was letting us know now because it would affect some of her functions with us.

Driving off the parking lot after that meeting, I heard the Lord say, "This is a 'marker' day."

Then I had a vision of a ship with lines like a Plimsoll line. It indicates the maximum depth to which a vessel may safely immerse when loaded with cargo. I often see these lines when going into the mountains of Mindoro in the Philippines. (There's a boat ride involved getting to the villages/mountains. It's a massive ship that holds cargo-people, vehicles, etc.)

Life can be so complicated and diverse in its unfolding. Things happen. Things change. But God put markers out there to help us see and to watch for landmines. Those are precautionary measures God provides so we won't get blown up or blow things out of proportion (if you know what I mean).

There are apparent markers that God provides to help us navigate our lives. When flowers begin to bloom, we know spring is here and summer is just a few months ahead. In the same way, God helps us look out for landmines for our safety. We need discernment. We need eyes to see beyond the surface.

Don't dismiss the landmines God put on your path. Detour is not always a bad thing. It saves lives…and it could be your very own life at stake.

Let's Pray

Father, thank you for being the only wise God!

Thank you for allowing me to depend on Your wisdom and trust Your word to be authentic and powerful.

Thank you for loving us in such a way that You would warn us or put markers along our path to keep us safe and sound.

Thank You for being our good, good Shepherd.

This I pray in Yeshua's name. Amen.

Our Decree

I decree our eyes are open and ears attentive to recognize the markers God has put along our path.

This I decree in Yeshua's name. Amen.

DAY 14

And He was also telling them a parable: "No one tears a piece of cloth from a new garment and puts it on an old garment; otherwise he will both tear the new, and the patch from the new garment will not match the old. And no one pours new wine into old wineskins; otherwise the new wine will burst the skins and it will be spilled out, and the skins will be ruined. But new wine must be put into fresh wineskins. And no one, after drinking old wine wants new; for he says, 'The old is fine.'"

Luke 5:36-39

"No one sews a patch of unshrunk cloth on an old garment; otherwise, the patch pulls away from it, the new from the old, and a worse tear results. And no one puts new wine into old wineskins; otherwise the wine will burst the skins, and the wine is lost and the skins as well; but one puts new wine into fresh wineskins."

Mark 2:21-22

Also see Exodus 17:1-7; Numbers 20:1-13

MOSES IS HERE (FAMILIARITY BREEDS CONTEMPT)

God does this to me all the time in the middle of worship. He speaks random words to get my attention. "Moses is here," He said.

Of course, the silly me scanned the room to look for Moses. Duh! I probably would've run out the door if I actually saw him. (LOL.)

But the message was clear. God was implying that we should learn from Moses' life. There's a lot to learn about him, but here are my most significant takeaways:

1. Pay attention to God's instructions.

God is pretty specific and leaves no grey areas when giving instructions.

First, He said to strike the rock for water to gush out (ref. Exodus 17:1-7).

The second instruction was for Moses to speak to the rock (Number 20:10-13).

Moses got familiar with how God does things and didn't heed the instruction the second time. The need for water may be the same, but the instruction given was different.

2. <u>Disregard of God's instruction could impair your future.</u>

Imagine your greatest pursuit is to make it to the promised land, but because you didn't follow instructions, it cost you your promise.

We cannot afford to repeat the same mistakes in this era and time. How we do things—our past experiences with God, how great they may have been—God may have already changed the game plan. Same vision. Same pursuit. But different instructions.

So, in the curve of change, remind yourself, "Moses is here," so you won't get stuck in the old pattern.

Let's Pray

Father, help! I despise the mundane repetition of things in this world called Christianity.

Teach me. Show me Your ways! Help me understand Your truth, not the lie this world calls truth.

I receive wisdom and revelation to help make this life matter in Your Kingdom.

This, I pray in the name of Yeshua. Amen.

Our Decree

I decree that the revelation of God's truth frees us from the bondage of religion and gives us the freedom to live freely in the Kingdom of God.

This I decree in Yeshua's name. Amen.

DAY 15

Come to Me, all who are weary and burdened, and I will give you rest. Take My yoke upon you and learn from Me, for I am gentle and humble in heart, and you will find rest for your souls. For My yoke is comfortable, and My burden is light.

Matthew 11:28-30

Now you are Christ's body, and individually parts of it.

1 Corinthians 12:27

WELL FITTED (YOKE)

In one of my travels in the Philippines, passing through a rice field, I was intrigued by some contraption on a carabao's neck (water buffalo) that I later learned was called a yoke. To us non-farmers, we don't see the significance, much less the use of a yoke in a farmer's life. In their world, however, it's perfect!

Jesus said to take His yoke and learn from Him; it's easy. He said, "Rest in Me because the yoke I give you is 'well fitted' for you."

It's custom-fit; it's tailor-made for you. My yoke- is specially made for you!

Think of the Kingdom of God like a jigsaw puzzle. God designed each piece to fit the exact spot where it is needed. Each piece looks different, but they create the whole picture.

There is room for you in the Kingdom of God! Each person is tailor-made for a specific task or function. Only when each piece is fitted appropriately will we see the whole picture. We must be willing to be fitted properly. This requires total surrender! We will feel like an outsider until we are willing to get connected. We will feel we "do not belong" until we accept where we belong.

In this Kingdom movement, we need each other. No comparing is allowed; only dying to self!

Let's Pray

Father, teach me to understand my place in the Kingdom. Help me to not compare myself to others, and help me be comfortable with how You have fashioned me.

Forgive me for thinking You made a mistake when I compared myself to others.

Show me how to embrace what gifting or skillset others carry, and help me be free from the bondage of people-pleasing.

Thank You, Father, for making us unique and helping us realize the need for each other to advance Your kingdom here on Earth.

This I pray in the name of Yeshua. Amen.

Our Decree

I decree that the Body of Christ, the true Ekklesia, is coming into her fullness.

I decree that each member of the Body is aligning and making the whole Body healthy and functioning as God designed for her to be.

This I decree in the name of Yeshua. Amen.

DAY 16

So teach us to number our days,
That we may present to You a heart of wisdom.
Psalm 90:12

My soul certainly remembers,
And is bent over within me.
I recall this to my mind,
Therefore I wait.
The Lord's acts of mercy indeed do not end,
For His compassions do not fail.
They are new every morning;
Great is Your faithfulness.
"The Lord is my portion," says my soul,
"Therefore I wait for Him."
The Lord is good to those who await Him,
To the person who seeks Him.
Lamentations 3:20-25

OLD WAYS WON'T OPEN NEW DOOR

Time and Change are two powerful realities in life that we cannot stop. Both are imminent, and we cannot control them. Whether we like it or not, tomorrow will come, and today becomes yesterday. Whether we realize it or not, we can never turn back the hands of time.

Accepting these realities is your most potent weapon to go about your life. That's why getting stuck in the past will not take you anywhere. Here are a few things I've learned over the years:

- You are a result of how you manage time and change.

- You are a product of how you use time and change.

- What you hope to become in five or fifteen years results directly from how you steward time and change.

- Time is a gift from God that helps fulfill your assignment.

- Change is a strategy to take you to your desired outcome.

Goal setting is noble and a great asset to keep track of your mission's progress. In the process, however, to reach desired result, you must be conscious of the changes in times and seasons. People and the environment change too. Circumstances change, and time does not hold still while things are shifting.

God's mercies are new every morning! He is faithful in providing us with fresh manna every day. Our Father does not run out of ideas to keep us sharp and healthy on our faith journey: mind, body, soul and spirit. We find an insatiable desire within us to want for more; yes, we do desire bigger things—most importantly, new doors and new opportunities.

Make friends with time and change. The sooner you embrace these realities, the quicker you free yourself from your old, stinking-thinking that has kept you bound in religion and frustration over the years.

Live Free!

> It was for freedom that Christ set us free; therefore keep standing firm and do not be subject again to a yoke of slavery.
>
> Galatians 5:1

Let's Pray

Father, teach me to number my days. Give me the insight to make each day count!

Forgive me for wasting time and for being a poor steward of time.

Help me welcome productive changes that I may advance in my walk with You.

Grace me to be pliable.

Shift my mind and unstick me from old ways and old habits.

I welcome Holy Spirit strategies to advance me in Your kingdom.

This I pray in the name of Yeshua. Amen.

Our Decree

I decree new wine in a new wineskin for the Church, the Ekklesia.

I decree she is advancing in the wisdom of the Lord and free from the old ways and the old pattern.

I decree that religion has no place in the Kingdom of God.

This I decree in the name of Yeshua. Amen.

DAY 17

The steadfast of mind
You will keep in perfect peace,
Because he trusts in You.

Isaiah 26:3

For though we walk in the flesh, we do not wage battle according to the flesh, for the weapons of our warfare are not of the flesh, but divinely powerful for the destruction of fortresses. *We are* destroying arguments and all arrogance raised against the knowledge of God, and *we are* taking every thought captive to the obedience of Christ,

2 Corinthians 10:3-5

Therefore, everyone who hears these words of Mine, and acts on them, will be like a wise man who built his house on the rock. And the rain fell and the floods came, and the winds blew and slammed against that house; and yet it did not fall, for it had been founded on the rock. And everyone who hears these words of Mine, and does not act on them, will be like a foolish man who built his house on the sand. And the rain fell and the floods came, and the winds blew and slammed against that house; and it fell—and its collapse was great.

Matthew 7:24-27

COMMON SENSE

In the early 2000s, my Pastor from the Philippines visited me and Greg while we were living in Amory, MS (Greg's hometown). Greg and I just pioneered a church, and I thought that was perfect timing for my Pastor to see what the Lord was doing through us. We were young pioneers, and his coming was reassuring for me.

We drove him around and showed him the quaint little town my husband grew up in. In one of our conversations, I decided to vent and get my pastoral fix from him. After all, that was the first church Greg and I pioneered together, and it was emotionally taxing.

I made clear that I did not mind the load of work I had to put in physically, mentally, or even emotionally. But it was the people that I had to deal with.

He chuckled (and may have snickered a little bit) and said, "O Joan, what do expect? If you have 100 people in the church, it's a given you're dealing with 100 different personalities. Some of them may even be demon possessed!" (The demon possess part was not a joke, either!)

My thoughts screamed: *You are not helping!*

Then it dawned on me: he was right! He was helping me realize that I must add a heaping dose of CS (common sense) into whatever I'm doing. Common sense says, "People are people." Some of them are fast, and most of them are slow! Heathens do what heathens know best to do. Christians? Unpredictable! One day hot, another day cold, and you can never please all of them!

My Pastor did me a huge favor. Pastoral care does not always come with a pat on the back. Sometimes, good sarcasm is an eye-opener. It just depends on how you perceive and receive it. It's like the two builders in Matthew 7. God sent them the same rain, the same flood, and the same wind, but they had two differing effects on their foundation.

Let's do ourselves a favor. Let's appreciate the simple little nugget of common sense. It'll free us from the burden of racking our brains out. People have different receptacles. People have different value systems.

We cannot make them all one and the same. Common sense says, "Deal with them according to their level of maturity, but remember, not everyone's mature."

Common sense, anyone?

Let's Pray

Father, I thank You for allowing me to learn from simple things.

Teach me to see things according to how You see and perceive them.

Give me the mind of Christ and show me how to take my thoughts captive when they become disobedient to Your thoughts and ways.

This I pray in Jesus' name. Amen.

Our Decree

I decree that we have the Father's eyes that see the good in things and people when good is not around.

This I decree in the name of Yeshua. Amen.

DAY 18

And everyone who has left houses or brothers or sisters or father or mother or children or farms on account of My name, will receive many times as much, and will inherit eternal life.

Matthew 19:29

Jesus said, "Truly I say to you, there is no one who has left house or brothers or sisters or mother or father or children or farms, for My sake and for the gospel's sake, but that he will receive a hundred times as much now in the present age, houses and brothers and sisters and mothers and children and farms, along with persecutions; and in the age to come, eternal life.

Mark 10:29-30

See Also Luke 14:25-33

COUNT THE COST

Who wants to count the cost when no one is even willing to pay it? That's a million-dollar question when talking about the D word: *discipleship*, or the cost of following Christ.

While there is much to cover on the D subject, I want to share my share of counting my cost in my journey of following Christ.

I became born again at 15 and was filled with Holy Spirit shortly after. I began serving at 17 and have not turned back since. Worship and travel were always in tandem growing up in the ministry. I was so focused on school and ministry that I didn't fool with boys, if you know what I mean. I was pleased with how my life was going; college, ministry and travel was a perfect scenario for me. There was no time for love until I met Greg at 26. He was a curveball, a good one, and I knew I had to bat this one and make a homerun. I did, and we're at 28 years with a lifetime to go!

A few days before our wedding, I sat on the edge of my bed and talked with Daddy God. I wanted to make sure I wasn't making the biggest mistake of my life. I wanted to ensure He was pleased with my decision. My Father's approval of every major decision I make is precious and a must-have for me. Since becoming born again, Father God's word has been the law I have inscribed in my heart. I knew in my knower that He approved of my decision, but He gave me a scenario that has become a metron for me when making big decisions—the passage of the cost of discipleship in Luke 14:

- Consider your cost.

- Count your cost.

- Choose your battles.

When you do this, pay the exact price, and don't forget to tip after, (i.e., go the extra mile).

Leaving my home, country, culture, father and mother, siblings, and friends too? What about the food that I love? No more dried fish? Oh, my heritage? My legacy? My identity?

What does it look like when God requires something of you? Be comforted in the truth that God always will outgive us. Plus, He is the best tipper in the world! The cost might be out of your reach. But guess what? Because He is such a loving Father, and a good one at that, there's always an attached blessing or inheritance to that request from Him. We have to trust Him…no matter the cost! It's always a win-win with God, even when you don't feel it.

Let's Pray

Father, thank You that I can rest knowing that You know best! When I miss home and family, You have never been short of making it up to me beyond my imagination. You've taken me to places where Your other family members from different tribes and tongues reside. You showed me that Your family—my family-is far more significant than I thought.

Thank You for loving me that way. Continue to teach me how.

This I pray in Yeshua's name. Amen.

Our Decree

I decree an ever-increasing family of God in the Earth!

I decree a selfless generation of believers that will traverse the universe for the sake of the Gospel of the Kingdom of God.

This I decree in the name of Yeshua. Amen.

DAY 19

I will ask the Father, and He will give you another Helper, so that He may be with you forever;

John 14:16

When He, the Spirit of truth, comes, He will guide you into all the truth; for He will not speak on His own, but whatever He hears, He will speak; and He will disclose to you what is to come.

John 16:13

Now Jesus had spoken of his death, but they thought that He was speaking about actual sleep.

John 11:13

And hope does not disappoint, because the love of God has been poured out within our hearts through the Holy Spirit who was given to us.

Romans 5:5

SHUT UP!

(I'M LISTENING TO MY FRIEND)

My invisible yet tangible friend, Holy Spirit.

I could relay many stories and experiences about Holy Spirit, but this one remains at the top of my list. Not too long ago, at an event, I responded to two challenging phone calls, and both shook me to my core. I hate those kind of phone calls, but I had to address them.

Just when I thought the fight was over, coming out of that private room, after I just squared my shoulders and fixed my crown, the enemy took it to another level. A demonic manifestation looked me square in the eye: accusation, defiance, fault-finding and unforgiveness since no apology was accepted. And mind you, manifested right in the middle of an ongoing event, coming from supposedly "trusted" and "mature" friends and a co-laborer.

From being shaken and stirred to being poured out, I was stunned. I felt like I had died from the inside. I was told by some of our leaders to quit apologizing because it wasn't my fault; that I didn't do anything. But I apologized anyway, still not realizing the reason behind the harassment. It took me a while to discover what was behind the madness. Later, I found out that they took out on me old wounds or offenses that they hadn't dealt with. A particular situation triggered something that they presumed I had instigated.

But Holy Spirit came to my rescue! I was able to shut the enemy's voice which rang louder that day, blaring more than the two phone calls I had just received a few minutes prior.

Silencing the enemy's voice in the heat of the battle takes focus coupled with courage. The ability to discern both what God is doing and the enemy's schemes to discredit God takes faith and yielding to Holy Spirit. He is our Teacher and Guide.

Most of all, He is our Friend.

I was told growing up not to say "shut up" to a person, and I agree. But I wouldn't think twice telling the devil to shut up anytime he opens his mouth! Again, not to a person or persons but to the demonic spirit manifesting through them.

Let's Pray

Father, thank You for being gracious to me at times when my flesh would've taken the best of me. I can't do it without You.

Teach me to die daily to self so that I may display the strength of Christ living in me.

This I pray in Jesus' name. Amen.

Our Decree

I decree that every offense on every level is uprooted and will no longer cause division in the Ekklesia.

This I decree in the name of Yeshua. Amen.

DAY 20

Now you are Christ's body, and individually parts
of it. And God has appointed in the church, first
apostles, second prophets, third teachers, then
miracles, then gifts of healings, helps,
administrations, *and various* kinds of tongues. All
are not apostles, are they? All are not prophets,
are they? All are not teachers, are they? All are
not *workers of* miracles, are they? All do not have
gifts of healings, do they? All do not speak with
tongues, do they? All do not interpret, do they?
But earnestly desire the greater gifts.

1 Corinthians 12:27-31

Also see Romans 12:3-8

THE "F" WORD

It's FLEXIBILITY, people, flexibility! (Get your
minds out of the gutter, LOL!)

We should never be stiff-necked! Life is too short to be a sourpuss. I mean, c'mon! This earthly life is ever-changing. Nothing is set in stone unless it's the gravestone that holds your cold carcass, six feet underground!

Ha! I can't believe I wrote all that! But it's true. When things don't go the way you planned them, it's not the end of the world. Now I know it's easier said than done. I get it. People react to things differently. People do not cope with change positively. But unless we embrace the reality that things can change right up to the last minute, we can play the blame game all we want, but it will not happen for us!

Administration or being administrative is one of my strongest suits, and it drives people batty at times. (Mainly my husband, LOL!) My high school awarded me the title Editor of the Year. (Who gets that kind of award?). They felt they had to give me an award because I was showing some leadership that wasn't on their radar. Simply put, I hated disorder and chaos and could quickly spot it on things and people as soon as I walked into a room.

Well, folks, you guessed it: I lived a life frustrated at everything! Did I say including everyone? It took me a while to discern that gift—it is a gift from God, after all—and to learn to steward it properly. The Greek for this gift is *kubernesis* and it means "to steer" or to "rule or govern." I was born a leader, and I can only humbly admit it. People saw those qualities, and I was the last to admit it.

The "F" word has been one of the most powerful tools in my tool belt since I recognized the responsibility of the gift I carried. It is a grace, not an entitlement. And because it is a grace, I must apply grace when responsibility calls. It must bend or flex when situations call for it, without jeopardizing vision and values.

Can it be done? Surely. As always, easier said than done. But it can be done, especially if you allow yourself to be flexible first.

Let's Pray

Father, thank You for trusting us with a gift only You can give.

I pray we will not, under any circumstance, misuse or abuse the gift You've given us.

I pray You give us the pursuit to be humble and not haughty.

I pray You give us the flexibility we need when there is a demand for it.

I pray for the mind and strength of Christ as we go about our daily business in life.

This I pray in Yeshua's name. Amen.

Our Decree

I decree that the Kingdom of God is advancing as every good and perfect gift from the Father is being used for His purposes only.

This I decree in the name of Yeshua. Amen.

DAY 21

Brothers *and sisters*, I do not regard myself as having taken hold of *it yet*; but one thing *I do*: forgetting what *lies* behind and reaching forward to what *lies* ahead,

Philippians 3:13

As far as the east is from the west,
So far has He removed our wrongdoings from us.

Psalm 103:12

But you are a chosen people, a royal priesthood, a holy nation, a people for *God's* own possession, so that you may proclaim the excellencies of Him who has called you out of darkness into His marvelous light;

1 Peter 2:9

See also *The Book of Hosea*

REFERENCE POINT

Our point of reference is crucial to our forward movement. It takes an intentional effort to change our lenses to see things in a totally different light. Failing to welcome this understanding prevents us from advancing in our lives, especially in our relationships.

When you hear a person's name mentioned, what are your thoughts about them? What are the bases of your thoughts? How old are those reference points? According to the *Oxford Dictionary*, a Reference Point is "a criterion, a basis or standard of evaluation, assessment or comparison to draw your judgment."

Forgetting what lies behind and being willing to look past an individual's seemingly old behavioral pattern requires a heaping dose of dying to self. It demands allowing God to forgive and love through you.

I struggle to trust people when their behavior hasn't changed and they repeatedly commit the same mistakes. I call them "repeat offenders," and it's the part of me that I constantly ask God for help. It cuts deep, especially when dealing with a loved one, a family member or a close friend.

The Book of Hosea is a good reference point for learning to love according to God's lenses. God depicted His love for Israel and all of us through Hosea. It's seemingly humanly impossible to marry a promiscuous woman like Gomer. But with God, all things are possible.

> And looking at them, Jesus said to them, "With people this is impossible, but with God all things are possible.
>
> Matthew 19:26

God's love is powerful! It is deep and wide and unsearchable. He can transform lives and wash them clean; white as snow! I'm sure you and I can say "amen" to that.

If you're reading this and can identify, know that God is rooting for you! It's not a burden meant to carry on your own. Don't give up! God can and will change people. You just have to allow Him. We typically err on trying to change people on our terms and our own efforts. My brain says, "God created people, and He can fix them!" Yet I have to intentionally move my emotions aside and let Him do the transforming

Easy to say but hard to do? Yes. But doable if you allow God.

Let's Pray

Father, You never shy at showering us with love and grace when we need it. Sometimes, we do not even recognize it. But thank You for being so loving and so kind to us.

Thank You for allowing us to love through You!

Help us forgive those who have wronged us, even if it meant the closest one to us who may have hurt us the most.

Teach us to clear our reference points about them.

Change the way we think about them, even as we allow Holy Spirit to change us.

Give us a new heart and mind when love or forgiveness is absent.

This I pray in Yeshua's name. Amen.

Our Decree

I decree that love triumphs over judgment on people and circumstances in our family, community, and country.

This I decree in Jesus' name. Amen.

21-DAY DANIEL FAST

21-DAY DANIEL FAST

WHAT IS FASTING?

Biblical fasting is giving up specific food and drink for a specified number of days, and could be for a particular purpose. While others fast because there may be a need or a Corporate "call to fast" they are joining, I fast from a perspective of pursuit and revelation—hearing God's voice clearly and our flesh subdued by Him that He may increase in us (ref. John 3:30).

Fasting, prayer and reading God's Word go hand in hand. When you fast, also pray for God's purpose and plan for your life to be revealed. Fast and pray about every major decision in your life. Simply put, fasting is a way to conquer the physical (natural realm) and open the door to the supernatural in your life. When you deny your body from its natural/typical desires, you feed your spirit and grow closer to the Lord. You're opening the door for the unseen to be manifested in the seen (ref. Matthew 6:10).

When you fast, you are open to God. Your spiritual capacity to hear and receive is increased. Fasting gives you breakthroughs in difficult situations because it draws from the power of God.

Myles Munroe

Why Fast?

In Matthew 6, Jesus gave us important insight into living in the Kingdom as children of God. He addressed three specific disciplines a believer must live by: giving, praying and fasting. Jesus said,

- when you give…
- when you pray…
- when you fast…

He made it clear that fasting, like giving and praying, was to be a regular practice or a given part of Kingdom life.

Daniel Fast – 21 Days

While there are several other types of fasting, we will only delve into Daniel Fast—a type of fasting that's common to many. It is the most frequently used example of a partial fast, and the book of Daniel, chapter 10, clearly describes it. The Daniel Fast is a type of fast that abstains from all kinds of meat, sweets, bread (carbohydrates), dairy, and drink other than water, abstaining from any caffeinated drink including drinks containing alcohol, for a specific period (re. Daniel 10:2-3). The easiest way to think of this fast is to eat vegetables and fruits and drink only water. One important thing to note about Daniel Fast is that you are not limited to a specific amount of food but rather to the kind of food you can eat.

But remember, you are fasting, *not* feasting!

> Please test your servants for ten days, and let them give us vegetables to eat and water to drink.
>
> Daniel 1:12

> I ate no pleasant food, no meat or wine came into my mouth, nor did I anoint myself at all, till three whole weeks were fulfilled.
>
> Daniel 10:3

GUIDELINES

How To Start Your Fast

Although fasting is a discipline or practice that doesn't necessarily require a goal (other than consecration to God), we can count on its benefits, such as seeing results on personal goals we set for ourselves or our corporate body such as Ekklesia (church) or parachurch or charitable groups. So, in this regard, you can:

- Start with a clear goal for yourself or your group.

Be specific. Why are you fasting? Do you need direction, healing, or restoration of marriage or family issues? Are you facing financial difficulties? Do you need to lose weight?

- Ask Holy Spirit for guidance
- Pray daily and read the Bible

How To Spiritually Prepare

- Intentionally set a rendezvous with God
- Confess your sins to God
- Ask the Holy Spirit to reveal areas of weakness or hidden sins
- Forgive all who have offended you Mark 11:25
- Ask forgiveness from those whom you may have offended (ref. Luke 11:4; Luke 17:3-4)
- Consecrate your life wholly to Christ and reject worldly desires that try to hinder you -Romans 12:1-2

What to Expect

When you fast, your body detoxifies, eliminating toxins from your system. This can cause irritability and mild discomfort, such as headaches during withdrawal from caffeine, sugars and other food or drinks you usually intake. And naturally, you will have hunger pains.

- Limit your activity and exercise moderately.

- Take time to rest.

Fasting brings about miraculous results. You are following Jesus' example when you fast.

- Spend time listening to worship music.

- Pray as often as you can throughout the day.

- Get away from the usual distractions as much as possible

- Keep your heart and mind set on seeking God's face and pursuing His heart.

How to End Your Fast

Don't overeat when coming to the end of your fast. Gradually start eating solid foods (meat). Eat small portions only, or snack on solids

Frequently Asked Questions

- Is fish considered meat?

Fish is considered pareve, meaning it's neither a meat nor a milk dish. It is kosher and passes the Hebrew practice of eating. Daniel Fast is widely practiced according to Jewish tradition & culture. I have considered eating fish because, according to Jewish culture, fish is not considered an animal.

If you have questions or are in doubt, listen to your conviction and the leading of Holy Spirit. For more information, Google fasting and Hebrew eating practices.

- What if I have a medical condition?

Consult your doctor before starting any fast. Decide together what is possible. If your health condition prohibits you from fasting food, try fasting something else and concentrate on prayer and Bible study. With Daniel Fast though, it will help you health-wise. But then again, be wise. Seek God before you do anything.

- I forgot and ate something I wasn't supposed to. Do I need to start again?

I don't think so unless you just want to. Think of fasting as a marathon, not a sprint. Conquering king stomach is complex, but you'll make it. Don't give up! We don't operate in legalism. We live by grace and under grace, so we don't abuse it either!

- Do I still exercise while fasting?

For most people, moderate exercise is OK. With Daniel Fast, you should be OK. But it is best always to know your limits. Consult your doctor if you have to.

- What if I have a manual labor job?

With Daniel Fast, you still eat, only not the food you're accustomed to eating regularly. If your job is physically taxing, try a partial fast that'll allow you to still get enough nutrition to perform your job. Again, it's on a case-to-case basis. You know you!

- Can my husband and I still be intimate during the fast?

Read 1 Corinthians 7:2-5, especially verse 5, which says, "Do not deprive one another (of sexual relations) *except with consent*, for a time; that you may give yourselves to fasting and prayer."

Scripture allows this for fasting and prayer, but only with mutual consent.

What To Eat During Daniel Fast

All fruits. These can be fresh, frozen, dried, juiced or canned. Fruits include but are not limited to apples, apricots, bananas, blackberries, blueberries, boysenberries, cantaloupe, cherries, cranberries, figs, grapefruit, grapes, guava, honeydew melon, kiwi, lemons, limes, mangoes, nectarines, oranges, papayas, peaches, pears, pineapples, plums, prunes, raisins, raspberries, strawberries, tangelos, tangerines, watermelon, star fruit, rambutan.

All vegetables. These can be fresh, frozen, dried, juiced or canned. Vegetables include but are not limited to artichokes, asparagus, beets, broccoli, brussels sprouts, cabbage, carrots, cauliflower, celery, chili peppers, collard greens, corn, cucumbers, eggplant, garlic, ginger root, kale, leeks, lettuce, mushrooms, mustard greens, okra, onions, parsley, potatoes, radishes, rutabagas, scallions, spinach, sprouts, squashes, sweet potatoes, tomatoes, turnips, watercress, yams, zucchini.

NOTE: veggie burgers are an option if you are not allergic to soy.

All whole grains. Including but not limited to whole wheat, brown rice, millet, quinoa, oats, barley, grits, whole wheat pasta, zucchini pasta, whole wheat tortillas, rice cakes and popcorn.

All nuts and seeds. Including but not limited to sunflower seeds, cashews, peanuts, and sesame.

Note: Nut butter, including peanut and almond butter, must be all-natural.

All legumes. These can be canned or dried. Legumes include but are not limited to, dried beans, pinto beans, split peas, lentils, black-eyed peas, kidney beans, black beans, cannelloni beans, and white beans.

NOTE: if canned, make sure there are no additives such as sugar.

All quality oils, including but not limited to olive, grape seed, sesame, and avocado.

Beverages. Spring water, distilled water or other pure waters, rice milk, soy milk, fresh squeezed juices or 100% natural juices without artificial sweetener.

NOTE: honey; natural gave; monk fruit, raw sugars, stevia or any natural-based sweetener

Other. Tofu, soy products, vinegar, seasonings, salt, herbs and spices.

Remember: Read the labels! No chemicals or artificial flavoring/seasoning.

What Not To Eat During Daniel Fast

All meat and animal products, including but not limited to beef, lamb, pork, poultry and all wild game meat.

All dairy products, including but not limited to milk, cheese, cream, butter

All sweeteners, including but not limited to sugar, syrups, and cane juice.

All leavened bread and baked goods.

All refined and processed food products, including but not limited to artificial flavorings, food additives, chemicals, white rice, white flour, and foods that contain artificial preservatives.

All deep-fried foods, including but not limited to potato chips and corn chips.

All solid fats, including shortening, margarine, lard and foods high in fat.

Beverages, All carbonated beverages, energy drinks, and alcohol, including but not limited to coffee, tea, and herbal teas

Coffee: Coffee is a bean. Unless you grind it, pre-ground coffee has added chemicals for a longer shelf life. Coffee has natural caffeine content, so we recommend limiting your intake during Daniel Fast.

There is a process to decaffeinate coffee naturally, but you must read the labels.

Tea/Herbal Teas. Decaffeinated vs. Caffeine-Free on labels. Decaffeination on teas suggests a chemical process, while Caffeine-Free suggests a natural process. How does all that work? I don't know. Have questions or doubts? Listen to your conviction and be led by the Holy Spirit. No judgment. No condemnation. Again, we live by grace and under grace. We don't abuse!

FOOD IDEAS

You may choose from the list.

Breakfast

Oatmeal

1 cup oatmeal (not instant) with 1/4 cup chopped apples, 2 Tbs. raisins, 1 Tbs. chopped walnuts and a pinch of cinnamon

Smoothie

1 cup calcium-fortified unsweetened soymilk, one small banana, 1/2 cup frozen berries of choice, 2-3 ice cubes; whip in blender 10 almonds or 20 pistachios

Lunch

Flatbread with Salad

3 cups fresh baby spinach topped with 1/2 cup sliced strawberries, segments of 1 small orange, 2 Tbs. Toasted sliced almonds, 1 1/2 tsp. olive oil and apple cider vinegar to taste

1 whole-wheat flatbread

Quick Mediterranean Platter

1 medium sliced tomato, one small sliced ball of pepper, 1/4 cup pepperoncini, 5 large olives, 1/3 cup hummus

1 1/2 oz. whole-wheat flatbread

Easy Veggie Soup

Simmer 1 cup chopped vegetables (such as scallions, carrots, and greens), 1/2 cup white beans and herbs to taste in 2 cups vegetable broth

1 baked sweet potato, 1 tsp. olive oil, rosemary or other herb to taste

Dinner

Pasta

2 cups whole-grain pasta

1 serving Easy Pasta Sauce

Easy Pasta Sauce

Saute 1/2 cup each diced bell pepper, onion, and one clove chopped garlic in 1 Tbs. olive oil

Stir in 1 (14.5 oz) can of tomato sauce plus herbs, salt and pepper to taste; simmer for 30 minutes. (Makes six servings)

Pineapple-Cashew Rice

Heat 1 tsp. olive oil in pan; lightly brown 1/4 cup drained crushed pineapple (no syrup); stir in 3/4 cup cooked brown rice, 2 Tbs. chopped cashews; top with fresh chopped cilantro to taste

1 1/2 cup steamed broccoli or snow peas

Corn, Black beans and Avocado

3 cups chopped romaine, 3/4 cup each canned corn and black beans, 1/3 of an avocado, 1/4 cup fresh chunky salsa and lime wedges

Snacks

3 cups air-popped popcorn

1 small tangerine/mandarin orange

1 whole-grain flatbread

1 1/2 tsp. natural nut butter

8 large olives

1/2 large whole-grain pita

1/2 cup chickpeas with a sprinkle of salt and 1 tsp. olive oil, roast at 375° F for 45 minutes, stirring often

<u>Trail Mix</u>: 1 Tbs. each raisin or chopped dates, chopped dried apple, unsalted nuts and sunflower seeds

<u>Mango Smoothie:</u> Blend 1 cup calcium-fortified unsweetened soymilk with 1/2 cup chopped, frozen mango, plus optional dash of cardamom

ABOUT THE AUTHOR

A 4th of July baby! Born and raised in the Philippines, Joan (pronounced "Jo-Ann") began her ministry journey at 17. She graduated from Far Eastern University with a Bachelor of Arts in Mass Communion. She completed her Masters and Doctorate degrees in Theology at Kairos Bible Institute in Waco, TX. Joan also earned her Master's and Doctorate degrees in Kingdom Studies through Kingdom University.

Joan serves as co-founder, Instructor and Chief Financial officer for Kingdom University, which now has 20+ campuses in the US and other parts of the globe. She also helps lead Kingdom Life Network (a Global Federation of Five-Fold Ministers and Churches). She also serves specifically as Co-Director for World Missions, covering Asia and the Pacific Islands.

Joan travels extensively and is passionate about seeing the Body mature, training Leaders and Infecting them with the Kingdom leaven. She loves to take teams into the nations and see them transform and "become" their God-given identity, seeing them thrive in their call and in their purpose. Joan is passionate about Missions and loves (to) Worship.

Married to Greg for over 28 years, they lead Kingdom Life Ekklesia in Franklin TN, where they also call home.

PREVIOUS WORK

Dr. Greg Hood

Praise for: *Sonship According to the Kingdom*

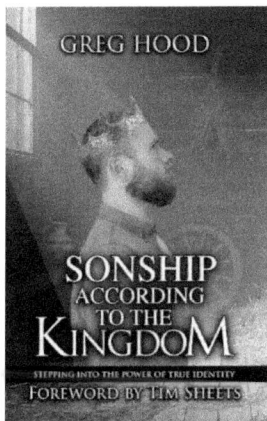

Sadly, many believers never come to a true understanding of who they really are in Christ. Paul rebuked the Corinthians for acting like mere humans. We are more than saved sinners; we are new creations. As sons and daughters of the Most High God, we're filled with His Spirit, infused with His nature, heirs in His kingdom, and partners in His great cause. You *will* come to a greater revelation of this as you read Greg Hood's powerful book *Sonship According to the Kingdom.*

Dr. Dutch Sheets
Dutch Sheets Ministries and *Give Him 15*

Praise for: *The Gospel of the Kingdom.*

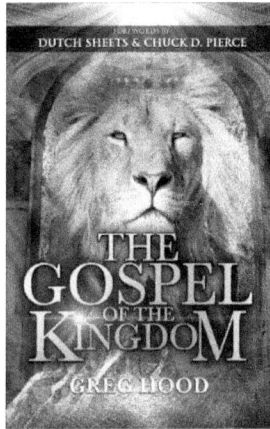

My friend, Greg Hood, is not only a teacher of the Word, but he is a student. Ever learning, ever maturing…as we all should be. The concepts and truth in this book may be new to you and that's okay. They are based on Scripture yet are just coming into their season. Kingdom, Kingdom Connection, Ekklesia, Apostles, Reigning in Life and so much more within these pages that will inspire you and encourage you and above all, change you. I encourage you to grab a cup of coffee, open your hearts and minds to what God is saying and doing, and take notes! Get ready to grow.

Tim Sheets, Apostle
Author of *Angel Armies, Angel Armies on Assignment, Planting the Heavens*
Tim Sheets Ministries
The Oasis Church, Middletown, Ohio

Praise for *Rebuilding the Broken Altar–Awakening Out of Chaos.*

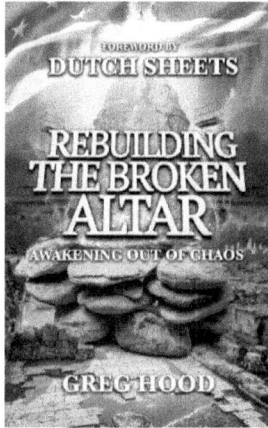

IF THERE WAS EVER A TIME WHEN a people needed to return to the Lord it is now. In his book "Rebuilding the Broken Altar" Greg Hood gives insight to the necessary process of recovering ourselves from the snare of the devil and experiencing the blessing of God again as a people. I would encourage, as you read to allow the Holy Spirit to stir your heart again with His passion for us individually and as a nation.

Robert Henderson
Best Selling Author of *The Courts of Heaven Series*

Praise for *Citizenship According to the Kingdom*

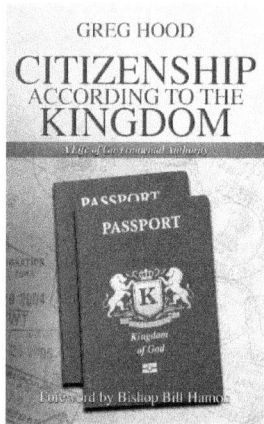

When Jesus died on the cross, he took our sin with him and left the concept of religion behind. Despite efforts to eliminate religion from our culture, some still strive to keep it alive. In recent years, I have come to believe that many in the Church have chosen to follow the rules of religion rather than seeking a genuine relationship with God. It's important to remember that only the sacrifice of Jesus can save us, not any religious actions.

Ricky Skaggs
15x Grammy Award Winner
Kentucky Music Hall of Fame – 2004
GMA Gospel Music Association Hall of Fame – 2012
Musicians Hall of Fame – 2016
The National Fiddler Hall of Fame – 2018
IBMA Bluegrass Music Hall of Fame – 2018
Country Music Hall of Fame - 2018

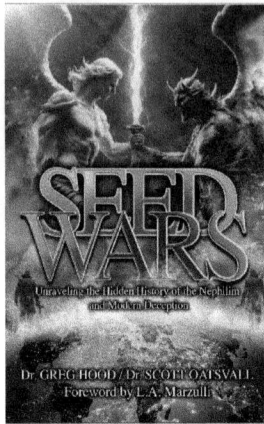

Every believer is called, like Joshua, to defeat the giants. In modern spiritual warfare we have associated these giants with spiritual strongholds and issues we must gain victory over. However, in *Seed Wars*, our eyes are opened to the influence of the original giants, called the Nephilim in Genesis 6, on our world. What unfolds in these pages will cause you to look at scripture, and biblical history with new eyes, and to look to our future with greater discernment.

Jane Hamon
Author of *Dreams & Visions, Discernment, Declarations for Breakthrough* and *Confronting the Thief*

KINGDOM
UNIVERSITY

DEGREE PROGRAMS

If you do not have a degree, you may obtain a degree in accordance with our academic requirements for Associate, Bachelor, Master, and Doctoral level degree programs.

If you have an earned degree, KU will evaluate your transcripts toward your next higher degree. KU can help you maximize your transfer credits and enjoy the benefits of a Kingdom Worldview.

NON-DEGREE PROGRAMS

Non-Degree Programs offer the opportunity to receive the same education provided in the Degree Programs. The student is required to attend in-person or online courses. No homework is required for Non-Degree Programs. Certificates will be awarded at the end of each year.

KU DEGREE MAJORS

In the colleges of Kingdom Studies, Five-Fold Ministry, Counseling, and Business, you'll be supported by faculty and administrators who are committed to your success. We have affordable tuition rates and we're military friendly! Eligibility requirements apply in each college.

DEGREES OFFERED

College of Kingdom Studies (CoKS)
Associates of Kingdom Studies (AS)
Bachelor of Science (BSKS)
Master of Science (MSKS)
Doctor of Philosophy (PhD)

College of Five-Fold Ministry (CoFFM)
Bachelor of Science (Theology) (BS)
Master of Theology (ThM)
Doctor of Theology (ThD)

College of Business and Entrepreneurship (CoB)
Bachelor of Science (Business and Entrepreneurship) (BSBE)
Master of Arts (MABE)
Doctorate (PhDBE)

College of Counseling (CoC)
Master of Science (Christian Counseling) (MS)
Doctorate (PhD)

INSTRUCTORS INCLUDE

Dr Greg Hood	Dr Dutch Sheets
Dr Jim Hodges	Dr BarbaraWentroble
Dr Patti Amsden	Dr Tom Hamon
Dr Jane Hamon	Dr Alemu Beeftu
Dr Tod Zeiger	Dr Scott Reece

Apostle Dennis Goldsworthy-Davis
REGISTER TODAY!! www.kingdomu.org
Contact us at office@kingdomu.org

SEE YOU IN THE CLASSROOM!!

www.ingramcontent.com/pod-product-compliance
Lightning Source LLC
LaVergne TN
LVHW021358080426
835508LV00020B/2339